Food Technology

Critical World Issues

CRITICAL WORLD ISSUES

Food Technology

Chris Banzoff

MASON CREST
PHILADELPHIA

Mason Crest
450 Parkway Drive, Suite D
Broomall, PA 19008
www.masoncrest.com

©2017 by Mason Crest, an imprint of National Highlights, Inc.

Printed and bound in the United States of America.

CPSIA Compliance Information: Batch #CWI2016.
For further information, contact Mason Crest at 1-866-MCP-Book.

First printing
1 3 5 7 9 8 6 4 2

Library of Congress Cataloging-in-Publication Data

on file at the Library of Congress
ISBN: 978-1-4222-3654-3 (hc)
ISBN: 978-1-4222-8134-5 (ebook)

Critical World Issues series ISBN: 978-1-4222-3645-1

Table of Contents

KEY ICONS TO LOOK FOR:

Words to Understand: These words with their easy-to-understand definitions will increase the reader's understanding of the text, while building vocabulary skills.

Sidebars: This boxed material within the main text allows readers to build knowledge, gain insights, explore possibilities, and broaden their perspectives by weaving together additional information to provide realistic and holistic perspectives.

Research Projects: Readers are pointed toward areas of further inquiry connected to each chapter. Suggestions are provided for projects that encourage deeper research and analysis.

Text-Dependent Questions: These questions send the reader back to the text for more careful attention to the evidence presented there.

Series Glossary of Key Terms: This back-of-the book glossary contains terminology used throughout this series. Words found here increase the reader's ability to read and comprehend higher-level books and articles in this field.

Introduction to Food Technology

Joseph Maloba is a farmer in the highlands of Kenya. For the last ten years, he has supplied a Western food company with green beans and has become dependent on their business. The company now says that the beans Joseph grows do not match its standards and has withdrawn its order, leaving Joseph facing financial ruin.

Joseph's Story

"My name is Joseph Maloba. My family has owned farmlands in the highlands of Kenya for many generations. In the past, we grew many different crops which we sold in local markets, but farming has changed greatly: About forty or fifty years ago, 50 percent of the money spent on food went to farmers; today that figure is much lower than 10 percent.

Today, food science and food technology are taught in universities and colleges around the world.

"Ten years ago, the company that bought most of my crops came to me with a contract. They told me they wanted my lands to grow only fine beans and insisted I use certain fertilizers and *pesticides* which were expensive for me to buy.

"They also wanted me to guarantee that I would supply a certain *tonnage* of the crop or face penalties. I had no choice but to sign the contract and accept their loan for the expensive chemicals.

 Words to Understand in This Chapter

blanch—to put food items in boiling water or steam for a short time.

convenience food—any packaged food, dish, or meal that can be prepared quickly and easily, as by thawing or heating.

deteriorate—to become worse as time passes.

enzyme—a chemical substance in animals and plants that helps to cause natural processes, such as digestion.

fermentation—a chemical breaking down of a substance, such as sugar, that is controlled by an enzyme and usually does not require oxygen. Fermentation typically results in the production of alcohol and carbon dioxide.

food science—the study of the physical, biological, and chemical makeup of food.

food technology—the application of food science to the selection, preservation, processing, packaging, distribution, and use of safe food.

microorganism—an extremely small living thing that can only be seen with a microscope.

pasteurize—a process in which a liquid, such as milk, is heated to a temperature high enough to kill many harmful germs, then cooled rapidly.

pesticide—a chemical that is used to kill animals or insects that damage plants or crops.

sterilize—to clean something by destroying germs or bacteria.

tonnage—the total weight or amount of something in tons.

The use of technology is expensive for farmers in Africa and other parts of the developing world.

Two years ago, I was told that my beans were no longer suitable. I could not understand it. They were healthy and tasted good. The company said they did not match their new standards—they had to be between 2-1/4 to 2-1/2 inches in length, 3/16 to 1/4 inches in diameter, and straight, not curved. The variety I grew was curved. These did not fit their packaging for European stores. My crop was rejected, and I had to sell many tons as livestock feed at a very low price. I am still paying back money to the company and am deeply in debt.

"I am fearful of genetically modified (GM) crops, but they may offer the only way that I can farm my lands again. One company has offered me GM seed for free for one growing season but only if I promise to buy their seed for many seasons to come.

"Many members of my family work at a processing plant preparing baby vegetables and tying them into small bundles with straw for supermarkets in Europe. The hours are long, and they are exhausted, standing on their feet all day. They are picked up by the company bus at sunrise and sometimes do not get home until midnight. They each have to prepare over 330

Food technology has been used to create foods that are ready as quickly and as easily as possible, such as this microwave popcorn.

pounds of vegetables each day, for which they get paid 220 Kenyan shillings (around $2.17). When I hear that a pack of these fancy vegetables sells in a Western store for as much as what a worker earns in a day here, I am filled with anger and am upset. How can this be right?"

Food Technology Defined

Every time you open a can of beans, reach into a freezer for ice cream, or buy a frozen pizza to heat in a microwave oven, you are experiencing food technology in action. Food technology is the application of science and technology to the selection, preservation, processing, packaging, distribution, and use of safe food. This includes creating food products, shipping them to stores and outlets, and selling them to consumers.

Our planet supports an incredible array of plants, animals, and other living organisms. Over a period of thousands of years, humankind discovered that many species were edible and could be hunted and caught, plucked from trees, or dug out of the soil and eaten in order for people to survive and flourish. Today, few foods are eaten as they are found in the wild. Most foods that reach the plates of people, especially those in more developed nations such as the United States and UK, have been prepared and processed using food technology.

Food Science versus Food Technology

Food science is the use of biology, chemistry, physics, and engineering to study the nature of foods. Food science looks at why foods *deteriorate* or spoil over time, how foods can be mixed or altered to create different food products, and how they can be

In the United States during 2015, 150 different food products were recalled from store shelves. Many of these products contained undeclared substances that were capable of causing dangerous allergic reactions in some people. In total, 21,104,848 pounds of food was recalled. Other reasons for recalls included harmful bacteria, unnecessary material, and processing defects.

preserved so that they last longer without spoiling. Food technology applies food science in practical ways to select foods, process and preserve them, and distribute them to customers.

Food technology is more obviously at work in highly processed, packaged meals such as *convenience foods*—also known as ready-made meals, prepared meals, prepackaged meals, or TV dinners—yet it also affects almost all of the food we eat. A strawberry bought from a store may look as if it has not been touched by technology, but the truth is different. Food technology may have been involved in many stages, from how the fruit was grown, harvested, transported, and packaged to the possibility that it was treated with radiation to increase the length of time it remains good to eat.

Food Technology Applications

Cheese is sometimes used as an example of the many different ways food technology works. In fact, cheese is an example of an invented food product. It is not found naturally in the world but is the result of a series of human-made processes. Food

Today, pre-prepared meals offer a wide range of menus, including many foreign or exotic foods, which can be ready in a matter of minutes.

The Inventor of Frozen Foods

Clarence Birdseye (1886-1956) from the United States invented a quick-freeze process in the 1920s. Working as a field naturalist in the frigid Arctic, Birdseye saw firsthand how freezing freshly caught seafood kept its taste and texture when it was thawed out and eaten several weeks later.

Setting up his first company in a New York fish market in 1922, Birdseye first froze seafood and then moved on to freeze meats, fruits, and vegetables. For people living far from the coast or farming areas, rapid freezing increased the availability of foods such as fish and vegetables. However, if vegetables are frozen directly, chemicals called *enzymes* cause a slow deterioration in color and flavor, even at low temperatures. To prevent this, most vegetables are *blanched* before they are frozen. This action destroys the activity of the enzymes.

Spreadable cheese is a food technology innovation that has proved popular with consumers.

technology often develops many versions of the same food by altering the ingredients and means of production. Cheese is no different, with 1,777 different types available.

Much of food technology's work is concerned with keeping foods from spoiling. Many cheeses are sold in sealed plastic packs and stored in supermarket chiller cabinets. Cheeses are often made from milk that has been *pasteurized* and may contain substances that prolong their shelf life. Cheeses have also been processed into new forms designed to be novel or easy to use in cooking to entice customers into buying them. The arrival of processed-cheese slices and cream cheese in a tube are examples of this aspect of food technology.

Origins of Food Technology

Tens of thousands of years ago, humans survived by wandering from place to place to hunt animals, catch fish, and gather foods from plants.

From around 8000 BCE, some peoples started to settle down in one place, growing plants and rearing livestock. The beginnings of food technology can be traced to this time in two different ways: First, early farmers started to note which individual plants produced the largest crop. By finding and saving these plants' seeds to sow the following year, farmers began to gain bigger harvests. Over many generations of selecting plants in this way, crop plants began to differ from their wild ancestors. Second, historians believe that wheat was one of the very first crops grown. Whole wheat grains are not very appetizing, but primitive food technology demonstrated that wheat grains crushed under stones could form a flour with which to bake bread.

Over time, people discovered how yeasts—types of tiny *microorganisms* used in food—could be added to bread to make it rise. Yeasts could also create alcohol from sugars and starches through *fermentation*—one of the first food technology processes ever to be developed. Beer brewing is believed to have been practiced since over 5,500 years ago in the Middle East.

Advances in Food Technology

In the past 150 years, advances in science and technology, a huge increase in the world population, and the rise of mass production methods in factories have all helped lead to more and more food technology innovations. The use of automated machinery in increasingly large factories has led to many foods being produced and processed in vast quantities.

The French chemist Louis Pasteur devised the process of pasteurization in the 1860s. Pasteurization involves heating a liquid, such as milk, wine, or fruit juice, to a relatively high

Modern food scientists are studying the genes of hundreds of species of plants and animals which are farmed to provide food for people.

Salmonella bacteria can be found on uncooked meat, particularly poultry. It can cause gastroenteritis. This results in nausea, abdominal pains, and diarrhea.

temperature, rapidly cooling it, and then storing it below 50°F (10°C). Pasteurization helps to *sterilize* substances such as milk by killing off microorganisms called bacteria, some of which are potentially harmful.

Plastics technology has developed to produce new ways of packaging goods. Canning, which stems from the early 19th century, and the rapid freezing process first introduced in the 1920s enabled foods which perished quickly—such as fresh meat, fish, and vegetables—to be preserved long enough to be transported around the world.

New foods have been created from scratch, while a variety of uses and ways of eating age-old foodstuffs have also been developed. One example of this is wheat and other cereal crops. Grown for thousands of years, crops like corn and wheat were first processed in the United States in the late nineteenth century into breakfast cereals. These products are now eaten by hundreds of millions of people every day.

 # Text-Dependent Questions

1. What were the problems that caused Joseph Maloba to end up in debt?
2. Describe four ways food technology is applied to cheese.

 # Research Project

Using the Internet or your school library, research the topic of convenience foods, and answer the following question: "Are convenience foods beneficial products of food technology?"

Some claim that they are good products because they have transformed people's lives—particularly those who are the primary cooks for their families—by allowing them to spend less time preparing and cooking meals and more time working or in leisure. Convenience foods do not stop people from cooking a proper meal if they wish; they just offer a time-saving option.

Others contend that convenience foods have a negative impact on society because many of them are higher in calories, fat, and salt than natural, unprocessed foods and can sometimes contain fewer nutrients. Because people buy so many processed meals, they often do not understand the need for healthy cooking or kitchen hygiene, leading to poorer health and more food poisoning, respectively.

Write a two-page report, using data you have found in your research to support your conclusion, and present it to your class.

Benefits of Food Technology

The world population has risen dramatically since 1950. In 1900, there were 1.6 billion people in the world, compared to 2.5 billion in 1950, and 6.9 billion in 2010. The growing population has brought the need for vastly greater food production, but innovations in farming and food technology have made this possible. Food technology has helped reduce food losses due to spoilage and waste in harvesting and transportation. Despite criticisms and concerns, food technology has also brought a range of benefits to many people, including increased choice, greater convenience, and lower prices.

Over a century ago, typhoid, tuberculosis, and cholera were diseases frequently transmitted through unsafe food and drink. Technological advances in food, such as the pasteurization of

Food has gone global—a head of lettuce can be growing in the soil of a Brazilian farm one day and tossed into a grocery cart in the United States three days later. Advances in computer technology and communications have combined with sharp reductions in the cost of transportation to transform the way food is sold.

milk and hygienic canning processes, have led to improvements in food safety that have helped conquer these diseases in many countries. Critics point out that other foodborne diseases remain, some of which may increasingly occur due to food technology practices.

Saving Time

Food technology has slashed the time people have to spend shopping for, preparing, and cooking food. In the past, most foods were *perishable* and had to be bought and eaten on a near-daily basis. Today, people can choose to shop far less regularly, relying on food stored in cans, dried packets, or in frozen form. Many foods are sold already prepared, so much of the kitchen work has previously been performed in food factories. Convenience foods, which only need reheating in an oven or microwave, have become a major part of people's diets. Euromonitor International reported $25.7 billion in US sales

 Words to Understand in This Chapter

disposable income—income that is left after paying taxes and buying things that are essential, such as food and housing.

irradiation—the application of radiation, such as X-rays or gamma rays, for therapeutic purposes or for sterilization of food.

parasite—an animal or plant that lives in or on another animal or plant and gets food or protection from it.

perishable—likely to spoil or decay quickly: not likely to stay fresh for a long time if not eaten or used.

A freezer full of pizza in local supermarket. In North America, consumption of frozen food has increased in recent years, mostly due to people's busy lifestyles.

of ready-made meals totaling 2.7 million tons of food. The largest consumers are aged 35–44, followed by those 45–54.

People today are looking to save money as well as time, and cheap, processed foods have helped to reduce the burden of the weekly food budget. The US Department of Agriculture (USDA) stated between 1960 and 2007, the portion of *disposable income* spent on total food by people in the United States fell from 17.5 to 9.6 percent. In 2013, they spent 5.6 percent of their disposable incomes on food at home and 4.3 percent on food away from home.

Expanding Choice

Food technology has increased the number and range of food products available to people in the more developed nations of the world. Food processing and preservation techniques, such as canning and freezing, have made many foods available year-round which otherwise would only be on sale in season. A century ago, few people in the UK would have eaten king prawns from the Pacific Ocean, while few Americans would have tasted items from the Indian subcontinent. Today, improved transportation and storage methods allow foods to go on sale which were originally grown or produced on the other side of the world.

Food technology has enabled foods and cuisines from different regions of the world to be packaged, promoted, and sold to consumers in Europe and North America. In the United States, for example, there has been a great increase in the num-

 The Food Industry in the US

The USDA reported the overall food industry in the United States—including farming, food and beverage manufacturing, supermarkets, and restaurants—contributed $835 billion to the nation's economy in 2014, 4.8 percent of the total. This included 17.3 million jobs, which accounted for 9.3 percent of all employment in the United States. Employment in food and beverage manufacturing, specifically, made up 14 percent of all manufacturing jobs.

According to a recent report, the typical supermarket stocks 35,000 different, items, much of it in a wide range of canned or pre-prepared foods.

ber of Chinese, Thai, and other Southeast Asian food products for sale in supermarkets. Hundreds of food products from Italy and the other nations in the Mediterranean region have also been produced to fill supermarket shelves in the United States, Canada, the United Kingdom, and other western countries.

Many products that we take for granted today—from dried pasta and canned sauces to baked beans and ice cream—are the result of food technology and its ability to create new products. For example, Quorn, made from growing and processing a fungus, is one of a number of new meat alternatives—including tofu and other soy products—that are now available to people. First sold as the filling in pies in 1985 after a ten-year testing program, Quorn is high in protein but low in calories, contains no cholesterol, and has a third less fat than a skinless chicken breast. Other commercial meat-substitutes include Boca Burger, made with soy protein and wheat gluten, and Tofurky, a turkey alternative consisting of tofu, wheat protein, and stuffing made from grains or bread.

Food Preservation

All plants and animals naturally start to change chemically and deteriorate after they have been harvested or killed. Food technology has developed many ways of stalling the spoiling process and keeping bacteria and other decomposing agents at bay. Preservation techniques include deep freezing and pasteurization reviewed in the previous chapter. Other methods include canning or vacuum sealing foods in plastic packaging so that oxygen in the air cannot reach the food product and cause spoiling reactions.

Drying or Freeze-Drying Foods

To thrive, bacteria require water, which is present in most foods when they are fresh. Drying food products to deny bacteria the water they need is thought to be the oldest food-preservation technique of all, stretching back thousands of years. Many foodstuffs today, from pasta and fruit to herbs and rice, are dried. This not only helps preserve the food but also reduces its weight, making it easier to transport without damaging.

Because heating food changes the way it tastes, freeze-drying foods have become a popular way to preserve them without changing the flavor.

Canning was invented by Frenchman Nicolas Appert in 1809. The process involves putting food into a can, heating it to kill off any microorganisms, and then sealing the can.

Drying rarely kills bacteria; it just prevents them from growing and spreading. As soon as the dried food absorbs water again, the bacteria can multiply, so the food has to be treated with care. Freeze-drying is a process in which foods are frozen and then held in a vacuum as the ice is converted into water vapor and removed. This complex process is relatively expensive but helps maintain good flavor and is used with more valuable products, such as instant coffee.

Irradiation

Irradiation is a method of preservation that uses a carefully controlled dose of radioactive waves, called gamma rays, to treat and help sterilize foodstuffs.

Gamma rays pass energy through food in a similar way to microwaves, but in irradiation, the food stays cool to destroy bacteria and *parasites* that can cause diseases in humans. Irradiation also kills organisms that cause food to spoil. Despite being passed as safe by the World Health Organization (WHO), USDA, and a number of other scientific bodies, many consumers have fears about eating food which has been treated with radiation, perhaps because the term is so often connected to hazardous nuclear material.

In addition to inventing pasteurization, the French scientist Louis Pasteur was the first person to prove that microorganisms are responsible for fermentation.

The Scope of the Food Technology Industry

The food industry today is the world's largest single industry, with over $4 trillion spent on food in 2012, according to the USDA. Technology has benefited the food-manufacturing industry tremendously. Food is now grown and harvested on

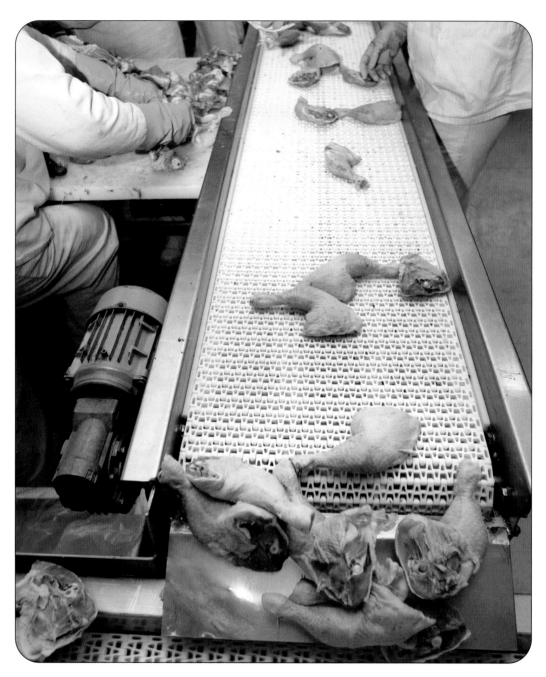

The presence of huge food processing plants, such as this chicken factory, mean that large amounts of food can be processed and sent to the stores in a very short period of time.

an enormous scale thanks to machinery and giant factories using automated processes that produce larger quantities of food products at lower costs. Preservation, packaging, and storage technologies have made it possible for companies to cut back the amount of food they waste. They also allow companies to buy ingredients from and sell their products to countries in every part of the world.

For many companies, sales and profits have soared, turning them from small businesses into giant multinational corporations with offices all over the world and sales measured in billions of dollars. Today, the 50 largest food-manufacturing companies in the world account for 26.8 percent of all packaged food retail sales globally. According to the World Trade Organization in 2016, the United States was the world's leading food exporter, with $175.57 billion in food exports, followed by Brazil and China, with $90.66 billion and $70.16 billion, respectively.

Changes in Buying and Selling Food

Less than a century ago, almost all food shopping was conducted in small stores and markets which served their local communities. Both the stores and their customers dealt in small quantities of foods, as the technology did not exist to store and handle larger amounts. With the rise of new ways of processing and storing foods in factories, stores, and homes, food products were increasingly handled in bulk.

The first supermarket, King Kullen, was opened in New York City by Michael Kullen in 1930 based on the notion that larger volumes of products would increase profits. Today, a few

A factory where tomatoes are being processed and canned.

large supermarket chains dominate food retailing in the more developed nations of North America and Europe. In the UK, for example, 80 percent of money spent on food went to small shops in 1950. In 2003, the same percentage was spent on just five supermarket chains. In the United States, 212,000 traditional food stores sold $571 billion of retail food and nonfood products in 2011. Of that total, the USDA found that in 2011, grocery stores, including supermarkets, accounted for 91 percent of sales, followed by convenience stores without gasoline (5.5 percent) and specialized food stores (3.4 percent).

These supermarket and food-manufacturing giants exert enormous influence on governments—as major employers—and on the consumer through huge amounts of advertising. They also wield great buying power over their suppliers. Most farmers, for example, are paid lower prices for their crops than in the past and are also pressured by food companies into growing specific crops at the right times.

 # Text-Dependent Questions

1. Name and describe three commercial food products that are meat alternatives developed through food technology.
2. What are four different methods used to preserved food?
3. What percent of retail sales in food stores are accounted for by grocery stores or supermarkets?

 # Research Project

Using the Internet or your school library, research the topic of the impact of supermarket chains on their communities, and answer the following question: "Are large supermarket chains good for communities?"

Some believe large supermarket chains are beneficial because they provide an enormous selection of food products at cheap prices. This allows customers to get exactly what they want and save hard-earned money, which makes an especially big difference for the poor. Chains also employ many people with steady jobs and draw more customers to nearby businesses that benefit from the increased traffic.

Others argue that supermarket chains destroy small businesses that cannot compete with the lower pricing or greater selection—some of these businesses have been local establishments run by families in the community for many years. This leads to fewer locations from which people can buy groceries, which can be problematic for people without vehicles. Chains have no personal connection to local neighborhoods because they are often run by corporate executives in other cities, so they do not care what environmental or social impact they have.

Write a two-page report, using data you have found in your research to support your conclusion, and present it to your class.

Concerns about Food Technology

T here are many concerns about how food technology affects the food we eat, including a number of issues surrounding GM foods that will be looked at in the next chapter. Many of the other concerns center around food safety and the impact of food technology on our health.

The Escalating Issue of Obesity

The typical diet of people in more developed nations has changed greatly in the past 50 years as food technology has led to a much greater availability of unhealthy, processed foods. Not only do people in wealthier, more developed nations have access to a greater range of products, shipped from around the world, but they also have access to a more abundant supply of affordable, easy-to-consume foodstuffs. Masses of people in

Sugar is refined in a processing plant. The addition of sugar to many pre-packaged and processed foods has contributed to rising health concerns, including diabetes, obesity, and heart disease.

these nations eat large amounts of convenience foods and other heavily processed food products, many of which contain high levels of fat and sugar.

Studies show that the populations of developed countries are growing increasingly *overweight*, with many people clinically *obese*—having excess body fat to the point where they seriously endanger their health. Obesity places a great strain on many of the human body's vital organs and functions. As a result, many people who are severely obese suffer from chronic health problems, including diabetes, high blood pressure, and, in particular, heart problems.

In the 1990s, for the first time in human history, the world's population of overweight people was roughly the same as the number of underfed people—about 1.1 billion. The WHO estimated that in 2014, more than 1.9 billion adults (39

 Words to Understand in This Chapter

allergen—a substance that causes an allergy.

biodegradable—capable of being broken down especially into harmless products by the action of living things (as microorganisms).

cardiovascular—of, relating to, or involving the heart and blood vessels.

emulsifier—a surface-active agent (as a soap) promoting the formation and stabilization of a mixture of liquids.

implement—an object used to do work.

obese—having excessive body fat.

overweight—weighing in excess of the normal for one's age, height, and build.

rancid—having a strong and unpleasant smell or taste from no longer being fresh.

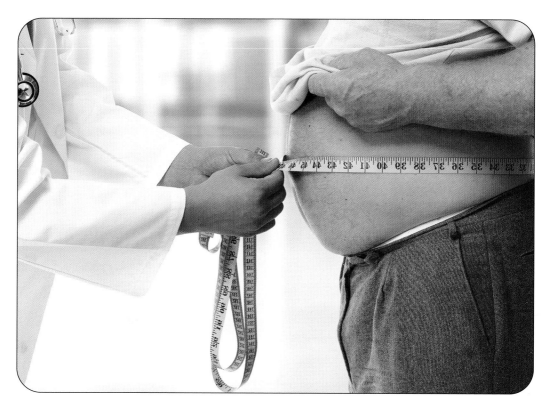

Some people blame obesity on the high levels of fats, sugars, and salts in processed foods today. A century ago, an average person would consume about four pounds of sugar per year. Today, the average person eats 160 pounds of sugar per year!

percent) worldwide were overweight and at least 600 million (13 percent) of these were considered clinically obese, doubling the obesity total since 1980. There were 42 million children under 18 who were overweight or obese in 2014.

In the United States in 2010, the National Institutes of Health reported more than one in three adults were obese, with the same rate for children. Obesity-related diseases—such as *cardiovascular* disease, cancer, diabetes, and high blood pressure—lead to 300,000 deaths per year in the United States. In

Many experts say the rise in the number of overweight people is partly due to the decline in exercise, as people's lives become more sedentary.

2014, the Centers for Medicare & Medicaid Services stated health care spending in the United States reached $3.0 trillion, or $9,523 per person. Of this figure, spending on care specifically for obesity was $190 billion, 6.3 percent of the total, which exceeds smoking in terms of cost for a public health issue. The economic toll is even greater when considering the number of work days missed or lower productivity while at work due to obesity.

Foodborne Illnesses

With so many food products available, transported such great lengths, food technology has made it difficult for countries and stores to ensure foods are safe for consumers. Foodborne illness, or food poisoning, is a risk whenever foodstuffs are produced and sold. Most food poisoning results in mild sickness, with an upset stomach and nausea. Some cases, however, can lead to severe health problems and, in extreme cases, death.

The WHO notes, "Access to sufficient amounts of safe and nutritious food is the key to sustaining life and promoting good health." However, unsafe food containing harmful bacteria, parasites, or other substances cause more than 200 diseases, including foodborne illness. Six hundred million people, 10 percent of the world population, become sick each year from contaminated food, and 420,000 per year die as a result—40 percent of these are children under 5 years old. Statistics from the CDC in 2011 show that in the United States, 47.8 million

 ## The Greatest Health Challenge

The Centers for Disease Control and Prevention (CDC) stated, "The most urgent challenge to nutritional health during the twenty-first century will be obesity." The International Obesity Taskforce echoed that sentiment for Europe, calling obesity "the biggest single European public health challenge of the twenty-first century."

In 2014, 1,700 people in Japan got food poisoning from frozen foods contaminated with the pesticide malathion. Japanese seafood company Maruha Nichiro Holdings had to recall 6.4 million products—1.2 million were recovered, but 5.2 million remained unaccounted for. The products, which included frozen pizza, croquettes, and pancakes, were found to have 2.6 million times the legal limit of malathion.

had foodborne illnesses, resulting in 127,839 hospitalizations and 3,037 deaths.

The vast majority of these cases are caused by toxins or poisons, which are produced in food by microorganisms. Not all microorganisms are harmful, and a number, such as yeast, are actually harnessed in food technology to help create food products as diverse as wine, cheese, bread, and yogurt. However, most incidents of food poisoning are caused by viruses, such as norovirus, or bacteria, including as Salmonella, Listeria, and Campylobacter.

Contamination in Food Technology

The key cause of most foodborne illnesses is poor hygiene, which lets food and food *implements* become contaminated with bacteria. Poor hygiene can exist in the home and in eating places. On occasion, it has been found to exist in the food industry as well.

Critics of modern food technology claim that because food products are manufactured on such a large scale, when food is

Poor sanitary practices at food-processing facilities can lead to the spread of foodborne illnesses.

contaminated, it can affect thousands of people over a wide area. Some people believe that with the many stages of manufacturing, packaging, and distribution that a manufactured food product goes through, there is far too much potential for contamination to occur.

Opponents also note that the many stages of food production make it hard to trace the point at which the food became contaminated. For example, in 1994, over 200,000 people in the United States became ill from eating Schwan's ice cream. After long investigations, it turned out that one of the tanker trucks used to transport the ice cream had previously carried raw eggs contaminated with Salmonella bacteria and had not been cleaned or disinfected afterward.

Food Allergies

There are 15 million people in the United States that have food allergies, including 9 million adults (4 percent) and 6 million children (8 percent). Food allergies occur when a person's immune system reacts to a harmless food substance as if it is actually harmful. The next time a person eats that food, the immune system releases large amounts of chemicals designed to protect the body. These chemicals can trigger a range of allergic reactions including rashes, hay fever, migraine headaches, asthma, and nausea. In severe cases, victims can suffer from breathing problems, a drop in blood pressure, unconsciousness, and even death.

Certain foods can be *allergens*, substances that cause allergic reactions. Eight foods account for 90 percent of all allergic reactions: milk, eggs, peanuts, tree nuts, soy, wheat, fish and

Some people are allergic to gluten, which is found in food made with cereals such as wheat, rye, and barley. They must eat gluten-free products, such as rice cakes, honey, and yogurt, which are becoming more widely available. This photo shows a shelf of gluten-free bread in a health food store.

shellfish. Even tiny amounts of a food allergen can cause a reaction, and these allergies tend to last for life.

Allergy sufferers strive to avoid eating foods containing allergens dangerous to them, but food manufacturing, which uses large numbers of ingredients, can make this difficult. For example, peanut products such as peanut oil are found in many foods, from dips and spaghetti sauces to cakes and ice cream. Sometimes, nut products that can be allergens are described on a food label as "hydrolyzed vegetable protein" or "groundnuts,"

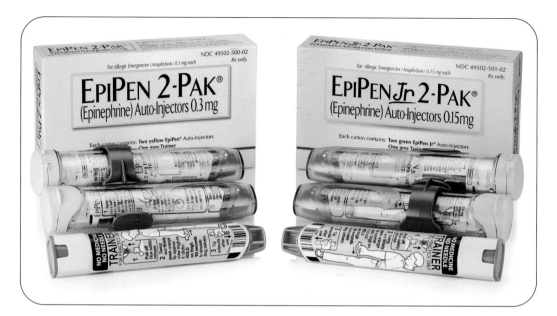

Many people who suffer from severe allergies to nuts or other substances carry an "epi-pen" like these. If they suffer a severe allergic reaction, they can quickly inject themselves with epinephrine, which helps to open their airways and blood vessels and reduces the impact of the reaction.

which are difficult to recognize. There may also be errors on labels or ingredients that are not identified. Some manufacturers cannot guarantee that their products do not contain allergens due to contamination from another production line or in the raw ingredients. Because of this, companies use unclear phrases like "may contain" as a warning on labels.

Food allergies are on the rise in the United States in recent years: In 2008, the CDC reported a 50 percent increase in food allergies among children between 1997 and 2011. Every year in the US, food allergies result in 300,000 child visits to the hospital and 200,000 emergency department visits for individuals of all ages. For children alone, the economic cost is $25 billion per year. There is no clear answer for why the rate of food allergies is increasing so rapidly, but critics point to the rise of the food manufacturing industry as a possible reason.

Food Additives

Additives are substances that are rarely foods themselves but are added to foods to improve the color, flavor, or texture or to help preserve a food's freshness or taste. *Emulsifiers*, for example, enable fats and oils to mix with water and form smooth textures in products such as margarine. Antioxidants are a type of additive that help prevent fats from turning stale or *rancid* while anticaking agents ensure powders like flour do not clump together.

All food additives in processed foods have to be approved by a country's food safety organizations, and strict limits are placed on the amount and type of additives allowed in foods. E-numbers are a coding system for food additives used in the European Union (EU), a collection of countries in Europe that share the same unit of money and many laws. For example, E102 is the code for tartrazine, which is frequently used as a coloring.

A number of artificial food additives have been directly linked to health problems, including cancer, asthma, and hyperactivity in children. A 2005 case in the UK involved a number of recalls for 576 food products that were found to contain a potentially dangerous coloring additive called Sudan 1. This dye was banned in a number of countries after it was shown to cause cancer in laboratory mice. The additive was traced back to its source in imported chili powder but had found its way into a wide range of food products, including herbs and spices used in pasta sauces and ready-made meals.

Natural Food Additives

While many additives are made artificially, some of the most common additives are natural substances, such as lemon juice, salt, and sugar. Other food additives are derived from fruits and vegetables. For example, tartaric acid is taken from fruit and is used to make some foods more acidic, lengthening the time they remain edible. Agar, extracted from seaweed, is another additive. It is used as a thickening agent and an emulsifier in many ice creams and canned foods.

Salt and Health

Salt (sodium chloride) has been added to food for centuries to improve taste and to help preserve foods—by killing bacteria directly as well as drawing water out of the food and depriving bacteria of the moisture they need. People need a small amount of sodium from food in their diet to maintain healthy salt levels required by the body.

However, too much salt in a diet causes the body to retain more water to dilute the sodium. This increases fluid in the blood stream, which puts more pressure on blood vessels and causes the heart to work harder. Over time, this pattern can stiffen blood vessels, leading to a heart attack or stroke.

Too much salt may also contribute to other diseases, including asthma. The Institute of Medicine recommends individuals consume less than 2,300 miligrams of sodium per day, but the CDC reported in 2012 that the average sodium intake for peo-

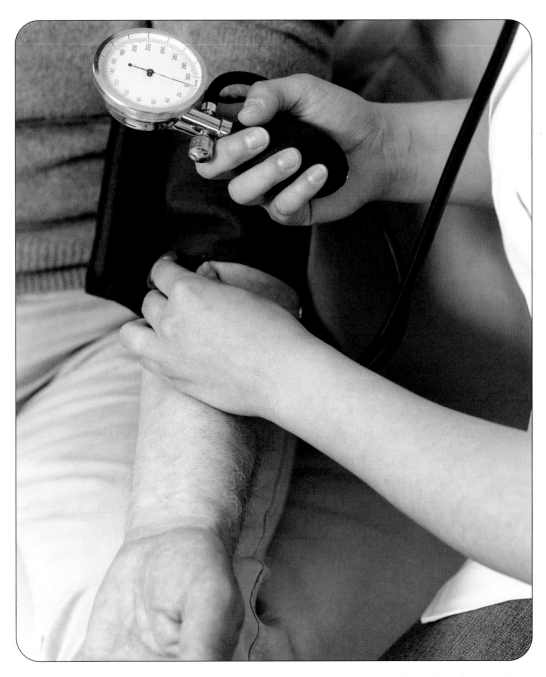

People suffering from high blood pressure need to avoid excessive salt in their diets and have their blood pressure monitored regularly.

Heart Expert Slams Salt

One cardiovascular expert in the United Kingdom stated, "People are much less aware [than in the past] they are eating salt, but it's all hidden in these processed foods. We are talking about foods that are 20–30 percent more salty than sea water. If we did reduce total salt intake by the recommended amounts, it would save approximately 30,000 heart attacks and strokes in the UK every year."

ple in the United States age 2 or older is more than 3,400 mg per day. Ninety percent of individuals in the United States eat too much salt, but a common myth is that most of it comes from the salt shaker in people's homes. Actually, about 75 percent of the salt people consume comes from salt added to restaurant meals or processed foods, where it is used to give foods flavor, remove chemical aftertastes, and reduce dryness. This makes it difficult for people to choose foods with less sodium, as they do not know how much salt they are eating.

Food Packaging

A century ago, people in many countries would travel to their local store carrying containers filled with milk and loose goods such as flour or sugar. Today, many arrive at their local supermarket by car, ready to fill the trunk with large amounts of

Packaging protects fragile products such as fruits, which can become bruised in transport and handling. It can also enable food companies to market and present more effectively to consumers.

A large vehicle at a landfill drives over a fraction of the household waste that has been produced by a single town. Much of the solid waste generated is discarded packaging of food items.

heavily packaged food products.

Foods are packaged for a variety of different reasons. In some instances, such as canned products, the packaging is essential to the way the food is preserved, or it helps promote food safety, as with tamper-proof seals. Other packaging is designed so that foodstuffs can be easily handled, transported, and sold by companies. Relatively fragile foods—such as fruit, tomatoes, cakes, and crackers—benefit from protective packaging so that they reach the consumer in perfect condition.

Packaging is also used to market and sell food to consumers. Millions of dollars are spent every year by food companies to create packaging that catches the eye of the consumer, makes the food more convenient to use, and gives a sense of safety about the product, which leads to increases in sales and profits.

Problems from Packaging

First and foremost, packaging uses vast amounts of the world's resources. Hundreds of thousands of trees have to be felled to provide paper and cardboard. Millions of gallons of oil are used to produce the many types of plastics and foams that constitute much food packaging. In addition, further resources are used to generate the large amounts of energy required for the packaging equipment in food-manufacturing factories.

Many consumer groups argue that packaging is deliberately designed to influence people into buying larger quantities of food than they actually require. Several studies in the US have shown that companies provide foods in larger quantities than a typical serving, which generates unnecessary waste and also encourages people to consume more than they really need.

Much food packaging is discarded soon after the food is bought or used, and this increases the problem of waste. According to the US Environmental Protection Agency, 251 million tons of garbage was generated in the United States in 2012, with 30 percent from containers and packaging and 14.5 percent from food waste. Much of food packaging is not *biodegradable*, so it permanently affects the environment if left in nature.

In the Los Angeles area alone, 10 metric tons of plastic fragments—such as grocery bags, straws and soda bottles—are dumped into the Pacific Ocean every day. The average person in the United States throws away approximately 185 pounds of plastic per year, with 50 percent of the plastic used just once before being tossed. Over the last 10 years, more plastic has been produced than in the entire last century, and enough is discarded each year to circle the earth four times.

The developed world is responsible for most of this waste, and managing it is a major ecological problem. Large areas of land are used for burying waste in landfill sites, and pollution is produced when waste materials are burned. The direct impact on living creatures is also serious, as 1 million sea birds and 100,000 marine mammals are killed every year from plastic in the oceans, and 93 percent of Americans age six or older test positive for the plastic chemical BPA.

Pesticides in Foods

Pesticides are used by farmers to prevent insects or animals from eating crops or spreading disease to them, but they can also be dangerous to human health if consumed. Washing fruits

A plane sprays pesticide across crop land to eradicate harmful insect pests.

and vegetables can remove some pesticides, but one study stated up to 60 percent of pesticides eaten by humans are "systemic," or taken up by the roots and distributed throughout the plant, unable to be washed off or removed.

According to the USDA's Pesticide Detection Program in 2014, 39 percent of canned green beans, 36.3 percent of bananas, and 32.1 percent of watermelons tested contained at least one pesticide residue. Of the cherries tested, 19.5 percent—about 1 in 5—had at least 5 different pesticides in them, and 9.7 percent of strawberries had at least 10 pesticides. Only

41.5 percent of all samples of foods tested had no pesticide residues. About 3.1 percent of carrot samples and 3.0 percent of summer squash were found to be contaminated with dieldrin, a pesticide banned over 20 years ago but still found in the soil.

Other Concerns about Food Technology

Many individuals and organizations are concerned that enormous food manufacturing and retailing companies hold so much power. This power, it is argued, is used to influence governments to prevent new safety measures and higher food standards from becoming law because they would cost the companies more money. A pressure group for higher standards may raise thousands of dollars in funding to promote their side of an issue, but against them may be one or more food companies with millions of dollars as well as influence in government.

Many campaigners say giant food companies also use their enormous buying power to exploit farmers and food suppliers, especially those in poorer, less developed nations. Joseph's story at the start of this book is typical of small farmers in many countries.

Other people are concerned with the way that large-scale farming demanded by massive food companies has profound effects on the environment. One example is the enormous amounts of pesticides used in large-scale farming. The pesticides not only remain as a residue on and in crops but also seep into the soil and through water runoff into streams, rivers, and lakes. Over time, a buildup of these poisonous substances can cause major harm to plant and animal life in a region.

Some people are uncomfortable with the methods that modern industrialized farming operations, such as this poultry farm, use to maximize production.

The giant American agricultural corporation Monsanto has become controversial due to its involvement in genetically modified foods.

Battery Farming and Animal Cruelty

In the effort to mass produce meat and dairy products, food companies often house animals in unsafe or stressful conditions in order to maximize efficiency and profits. Many people believe that battery farming—keeping egg-laying hens in rows of small cages stacked on top of each other—is one of a number of farming methods that are cruel to animals. Battery farming was developed in the United States in the 1930s and requires fewer people to tend the chickens. The largest such farms in the UK house over 80,000 chickens in cages that are stacked many rows high. Each hen rarely has more than 70 square inches of living space, which is about the size of an 8.5-by-11-inch sheet of paper. Birds in these cramped spaces are unable to stretch, spread their wings, or clean themselves properly.

 # Text-Dependent Questions

1. Provide three statistics that speak to the problem of obesity that the food industry contributes to.
2. How does salt affect human health, and what are the two sources for most of the salt people consume?
3. Name two negative consequences of packaging waste from food products.

 # Research Project

Using the Internet or your school library, research the topic of obesity and convenience foods, and answer the following question: "Is food technology to blame for rising obesity in the world?"

Some think that food technology is to blame because it has created many convenience foods that are high in fat and calories—proven causes of obesity. These foods are more tempting to the consumer, so food manufacturers achieve higher sales. By making such unhealthy products widely available and cheap, food companies are being irresponsible with people's health in order to make greater profits. If they provided healthier choices, obesity rates would decrease, but companies would have to be willing to make less money.

Others say it is the consumer's responsibility to eat a healthy, balanced diet, which can include moderate amounts of convenience foods. Food manufacturers provide options, but they do not force people to choose them. In addition, there are other factors, such as getting less exercise, which contribute to obesity that are also dependent on people's choices. Food technology did not create the first high-calorie, high-fat products. Some, such as peanuts, already existed in nature, and people would still eat those if convenience foods were not available.

Write a two-page report, using data you have found in your research to support your conclusion, and present it to your class.

4

Genetically Modified Foods

Inside the cells of living things, *genes* guide how living things are made and how they function. After decades of research in *genetic engineering*, scientists have learned how to alter the individual genes—the parts of cells that control the characteristics of a living thing—of many different species of living things in order to create new varieties with desirable characteristics. Much of the research has been focused on creating GM crops and animals for food, and the topic of GM foods has aroused passionate debate, both for and against.

Altering plants and animals is not a new innovation. For many centuries, in a process called *selective breeding*, people

An American protester holds a sign showing how she feels about GMO foods during a "March Against Monsanto" rally in Pensacola, Florida.

have been breeding plants and creating hybrids by crossing them to create a new variety. The world's main food crops—such as wheat, barley, and potatoes—have all been selected, crossed, and bred to suit the conditions in which they are grown, produce greater quantities at harvest time, and make them tastier. The same has occurred with animals. Cattle, for example, have been selectively bred over many centuries to create varieties that yield large quantities of meat or milk. The herds of beef and dairy cattle that exist today vary greatly from one other as well as from the cattle that existed thousands of years ago.

 Words to Understand in This Chapter

DNA—deoxyribonucleic acid: a molecule that carries genetic information in the cells of plants and animals.

field trial—a trial of a new product in actual situations for which it is intended.

genes—a part of a cell that controls or influences the appearance, growth, etc., of a living thing.

genetic engineering—the science of making changes to the genes of a plant or animal to produce a desired result.

GMO—genetically modified organism: a plant or animal whose genetic material has been altered by genetic engineering.

herbicide—a chemical used to destroy plants or stop plant growth.

organic—grown or made without the use of artificial chemicals or GMOs.

selective breeding—the intentional mating of two animals or plants in an attempt to produce offspring with desirable characteristics or for the elimination of a trait.

unequivocal—very strong and clear, not showing or allowing any doubt.

DNA

Living things are made up of millions of tiny cells, inside each of which is the genetic information that dictates what the living thing will be and what characteristics it will have. This genetic material comes in a sequence of codes in a molecule called deoxyribonucleic acid (*DNA*). In 1953, James Watson and Francis Crick discovered that DNA looks like a long ladder twisted into the shape of a corkscrew called a double-helix. Scientists have discovered ways to manipulate the DNA directly to create GM plants and animals.

Genetic Modification versus Selective Breeding

Selective breeding requires many generations of parents and offspring. It takes many years, even centuries, to produce the desired results. Genetic engineering, on the other hand, is very fast: altering the genes in a laboratory can be done in a few weeks, or even days, and all within one generation.

Traditional plant and animal breeding involves mixing thousands of genes contained within two plants or animals that are bred or crossed. It uses the natural mating process of two individuals of the same species, so genes can only be altered within the same species.

In genetic modification, on the other hand, scientists have developed the ability to switch individual genes on or off in cells, and they can also insert a gene from one species into a

Over the years, apples have been crossed and bred to create the huge number of varieties available today.

completely different one. For example, scientists have added a gene that is found in the cold-water flounder fish into the genetic makeup of a tomato. In the flounder, the gene makes an antifreeze chemical that enables it to survive cold conditions. The resulting tomato has been shown to be more frost-resistant than traditional tomatoes.

Spread of GM Crops

In 2014, there were 181.5 million hectares of GM crops worldwide, compared to 90 million hectares in 2005 and just 1.7 million hectares in 1996—a 100-fold increase in 18 years. Eighteen million farmers are growing GM crops today.

A 2014 report by the International Service for the Acquisition of Agri-Biotech Applications (ISAAA) showed five countries make up most of the GM crop area in the world—the United States (73.1 million hectares), Brazil (42.2 million), Argentina (24.3 million), India (11.6 million), and Canada (11.6 million).

The Many Forms of Soy

Food technologists have learned how to process crops like soy into a variety of forms, including soy milk, soy oil, and soy protein which is used as a meat substitute. Soy is also a source of lecithin, found in many foods—from sauces to chocolate—where it is used as a thickener.

The four main GM crops are soybean, cotton, maize, and rapeseed (canola). In 2014, GM crops made up 82 percent of the 111 million hectares of the soybean planted globally; 68 percent of the 37 million hectares of cotton; 30 percent of the 184 million hectares of maize; and 25 percent of the 36 million hectares of canola.

However, by no means are all GM crops being grown by ordinary farmers in ordinary fields as food for people. Some are still being researched while others are being test-grown in greenhouses or in *field trials*—tests in real conditions—on small, carefully controlled plots of land. The USDA allowed testing on 4 GM crops in 1985, 1,194 in 2002, and over 12,000 in 2013.

Savor the Flavor

One of the first genetically-engineered foods to go on sale to the public was the Flavr-Savr tomato. It was introduced into 730 stores in the United States in late 1994. It had been engineered to stay fresh on the shelf for a longer time than the average tomato, holding its flavor well instead of becoming squishy and rotten. But opposition from farmers and consumers, along with problems growing the tomatoes on a large scale, eventually fed to the Flavr-Savr being withdrawn from the market.

Benefits of GM Crops

Genetic engineering can create crops that are resistant to *herbicides,* so the sprays can be used to kill weeds without harming the crop. It can allow crops to produce a substance that will deter insects from eating them or make crops resistant to diseases caused by plant viruses. Genetic engineering can also improve the quality and quantity of crops, giving them the advantages of faster growth, bigger yields, and better flavor.

Genetic engineering might allow plants to grow in a wider range of growing conditions. If GM wheat could grow in drier soil or survive a short drought, it might grow in places where *organic* wheat—grown without artificial chemicals or genetically modified organisms (*GMOs*)—cannot survive. Food could then be produced in former areas of famine and feed multitudes of hungry people.

Certain genes can control ripening, so all of a GM crop can be ready to harvest at the same time. Other genes can make soft fruits less prone to damage, marks, and bruises as they are picked, packed, transported, and put on display.

The appearance of a food plant can also be changed, so that apples look shiny and smooth rather than dull and wrinkled. It might even be possible to change the colors of plants and animals by genetic engineering and create "novelty" foods such as blue tomatoes or red peas!

Golden Rice

Rice is the main food for more than half of the world's people. A GM variety called "golden rice" is designed to provide the body with more vitamin A. The WHO estimates 250 million preschool-aged children have vitamin A deficiency, which is the leading cause of preventable blindness in children. Golden rice could provide millions with the vitamin A they need. Field trials began in Louisiana in 2004, and in 2005, a newly engineered version was found to contain even more nutrients than the previous version.

Studies continue to be conducted for effectiveness and safety, but there has been opposition along the way: Some say researchers gave test subjects unnatural, higher-fat diets, so the

A child stands in a field of golden rice in Thailand. As the world's population continues to grow, some experts hope that high-yield GM foods may help alleviate hunger while also reducing the strain on natural resources due to overfishing and other environmental issues.

vitamin A levels would come out higher. Others claimed the tests were unethically done on children whose parents did not know the rice was a GM crop or that it was under trial. Many believe that the poor are used as a reason for GM crop development when in fact large corporations are seeking huge profits from GM products like golden rice.

Potential Risks of GM Foods

In theory, it is possible that new genes put into food plants and animals could damage the human body. Though there have been differing studies, there has not been *unequivocal* evidence that any GM foods are harmful to humans. GM foods in the United States also have to be approved by the Food and Drug Administration (FDA), but that does not mean that safety is always guaranteed.

Genes added to a food product, such as a farm crop, are intended to have certain effects, but they might also have other, unexpected effects: They could cause the plant to produce extra amounts of its natural chemicals. In normal amounts these cause no problems, but larger amounts might be poisonous. Or the new genes might make the plant produce unexpected substances which could be toxic or cause allergies. For example, a type of GM corn that produces its own pesticide was believed just to kill pests, but research has shown that it may also kill caterpillars of the harmless Monarch butterfly. In addition to the risks to animals, what if this happened with humans?

Supporters of genetic engineering argue that millions of people have been eating GM foods for many years, and there are still no proven cases of direct harm being caused. Also, GM foods undergo extensive testing before distribution to the public. These trials are conducted in the laboratory, on animals, and on people who volunteer. Indeed, GM foods are tested far more than those made by traditional methods of selective breeding and have been found to be safe.

Identifying GM Foods

It can be relatively simple to identify "single" GM food products such as GM potatoes, oranges, or chickens. Many producers and supermarkets in the world already label them, so the consumer can choose whether or not to eat them. But foodstuffs such as maize and soy are bought, sold, mixed, and blended several times before being used as ingredients in sauces, gravies, pies, fillings, pizzas, and ready-made meals. It is not always easy, or even possible, to know if a processed or ready-made item contains GM foodstuffs. The United States currently has no requirement to label these products, and while this may come in the future, doing so may increase the price of foods.

Genes in the Wild

In most crops, the male parts of a flower release thousands of tiny pollen grains. They are blown by the wind or carried by creatures such as bees or birds to the female parts of a flower of the same species. A male cell in the pollen grain joins with a female cell in the flower to start the development of a new seed.

It is possible that male pollen grains from a GM plant could reach the female parts of a natural plant of the same species in another field. The new genes might get into the seeds of that plant and then be spread again by the pollen. In this way, the new gene could travel long distances, perhaps even across continents. The new gene might spread to the original wild version of the plant and change nature forever.

As we farm GM animals for food, it might turn out to be impossible to keep the "GMs" away from the "organics." A GM animal might interbreed with an organic one, allowing the new gene to gradually "escape" into the wild and spread into the

The feelings against the growth of genetically modified organisms has led to a rise in the number of anti-GMO organizations around the globe, as well as protests like this one in Canada.

natural population. The effects are unpredictable, so precautions are taken to prevent this from happening.

Scientists and farmers in the United States must go through several steps to test GM foods for safety in a controlled environment. At first, a new GM plant, such as GM wheat, is grown in a laboratory and then in larger numbers in a greenhouse. Plants are carefully studied to see if their growth is healthy and whether they produce any unusual new substances. Their useful parts, such as the grains in wheat, are tested for ill-effects by feeding them to animals.

After the initial tests and studies have been completed for safety, the GM crop is grown in small batches in field trials.

Those who operate organic farms are generally proud that their food crops are grown "the natural way," but they may worry that pollen from genetically modified (GM) crops grown on nearby farms might be carried on the wind and affect their own crops.

Genetically modified foods are studied carefully in the contained, controlled surroundings of a greenhouse. This helps to reduce the risks of genes escaping into the environment.

These field trials have to be carried out a certain distance from any non-GM fields of that crop. But studies show that some pollen grains can blow on the wind for at least 30 miles, and birds and bees can spread seeds and pollen even farther afield.

Possible Consequences of Escaped Genes

The possibility that a gene might transfer from a properly tested GM plant or animal into natural populations of plants and animals is exceedingly small. But the possible consequences, if this

These Afghan boys are harvesting potatoes. Farmworkers in many developing countries of Asia, Africa, and South America have to work hard to grow crops in tough conditions. Many people argue that GM plants will provide crops which are easier to grow, making farmers' lives easier.

did occur, are far reaching. In a laboratory or greenhouse, there is an excellent chance of restricting the spread of a gene. But in the outside world, little can be done to halt it or get it back.

Suppose that a GM crop has a gene to resist a certain weed-killer spray. Out in the field, the crop suffers from a disease caused by a virus. Some of the viruses take up the gene from the crop and infect a weed nearby, passing the gene to the weed. The weed might then become a "super weed," resistant to the weed killer, and spread to cause huge damage. The exact same process of "carrier" viruses transferring genes from one type of living thing to another is used in genetic engineering itself.

Imagine another case involving animals: A "super pig" gene causes baby pigs to grow much bigger and faster. One day, one escapes and breeds with its natural cousin, the wild boar. The gene is passed, stage by stage, into the local wild boar population. This creates a new breed of "super boar" that wreaks havoc on the environment.

Genetic-engineering supporters argue that the chances of genes escaping, jumping to other living things, and then actually working in them are so small as to be almost zero. But opponents compare the risk to the myth of the genie in the bottle: the genie promises to grant wishes, but the person who makes the wish does not think of all the possible consequences until it is too late.

Opponents of genetic engineering say that once a new gene has escaped into nature, it can never be recaptured. Super weeds might smother the land, super bugs may spread plagues, and super animals could endanger lives. You cannot put the genie, or the gene, back in the bottle.

Anti-GMO Campaigns

In 1999 at several sites in the UK, anti-GM campaigners disrupted field trials of GM maize, chopping down and burning the plants. The field trials were legal and following testing guidelines, but the protesters said the trials had been hushed up, and the dangers of the trials had not been resolved. In court, no protesters were found guilty of any offense.

Protests have continued to the present day. In 2012, hundreds of farmers in India gathered in peaceful protest of GM corn, not wanting their fields to be used for testing. They cited other countries where super weeds have spread as a result of genes from GM corn that are resistant to herbicides. In 2013, 400 protesters charged a field in the Philippines, where a field trial of the aforementioned golden rice was taking place. They uprooted and trampled the rice plants, saying the GM rice trial was a danger to human health and limiting to the natural diversity of crops.

The Power of the GM Food Industry

Critics fear the power that a few giant GM-food companies could hold over the entire food industry. Food and Water Watch stated in 2009, 93 percent of all soybeans and 80 percent of all corn in the US were grown with seeds from just one company, Monsanto. Monsanto's products are grown on 40 percent of US crop acreage and on 282 million acres worldwide.

Powerful GM-food companies like Monsanto have enormous power when they control so much of the market. When options are limited, companies are able to control prices of seeds without much fear of farmers choosing to go to the competition. They might also insist on farmers paying a technology fee to buy GM seeds. A company can tie farmers to only their products by developing crops that are specifically resistant to pesticides made by the same GM-food company.

 ## Text-Dependent Questions

1. What are three ways GM crops can benefit people?
2. Provide one plant and one animal example of the risks of "escaped genes."

 ## Research Project

Using the Internet or your school library, research the topic of GM foods, and answer the following question: "Are huge GM-food companies good for society?"

Some contend that giant GM-food companies help society by creating more nutritious crops that taste better and last longer through genetic engineering. Selective breeding is essentially the same process, except it takes much longer and is not as specific in producing results. Large GM-food companies have the resources to research, test, and produce the best products, which can be grown in areas of famine or give needed vitamin-rich foods to the malnourished.

Others argue that large GM-food companies are not good for society because they force farmers to work the same amount but make much less money because of the costs of GM seeds and technology fees. These companies engineer crops and animals that can spread genes unintentionally into the wild, and who knows what the consequences may be of such irresponsible actions. Also, in the testing stages, human subjects can be manipulated or not even informed they are eating GM foods that have not yet been proven to be safe.

Write a two-page report, using data you have found in your research to support your conclusion, and present it to your class.

Nutrition Facts

Serving Size 1/4 Cup (30g)
Servings Per Container About 38

Amount Per Serving

Calories 200   Calories from Fat 150

	% Daily Value
Total Fat 17g	26%
Saturated Fat 2.5g	13%
Trans Fat 0g	
Cholesterol 0mg	0%
Sodium 120mg	5%
Total Carbohydrate 7g	2%
Dietary Fiber 2g	8%
Sugars 1	
Prot	

Regulation of the Food Industry

Every country has laws and agencies designed to ensure that the food their people eat is safe, produced in acceptable ways, and meets the standards set. However, many examples of bad practice in the food industry still occur, and these have helped prompt the rise of many pressure groups. These groups strive to make the public aware of food technology issues and campaign to make food safer for the public.

Food manufacturers spend millions of dollars every year on food hygiene and safety. Many companies use a system called Hazard Analysis and Critical Control Points (HACCP), which identifies the key stages in food production where food hazards can occur, so measures can be introduced to monitor quality and check for risks. The food that is sold to people in more

Government-required nutrition labels carry a lot of information, including the contents of the food, how best to store it, and even serving suggestions. Some people feel that adding more details would only confuse consumers.

developed nations is also governed by many laws that are enforced by hygiene and food safety inspectors and agencies. In the UK, for instance, Environmental Health Officers (EHOs) visit food industry factories and retail outlets, investigating complaints and checking on levels of hygiene and safe storage. Failure to reach standards can lead to court cases, fines, and products being banned.

However, many believe that food companies get away with thousands of *illicit* practices or, if caught, are punished too lightly. Critics argue that compared to the millions of dollars large food companies make every day, a fine of a few thousand dollars will have little impact. In 2003, new food safety laws were proposed for the countries of the EU that were far stricter than before. These laws proposed that farmers and food retailers could be jailed or have their businesses shut down if they broke new laws on, for example, trying to sell food with banned or unsafe levels of additives or pesticides. Making these new proposals law is one thing, but managing to enforce them is quite another.

 Words to Understand in This Chapter

central nervous system—the part of the nervous system that includes the brain and spinal cord.

illicit—not allowed by law: unlawful or illegal.

intensive farming—a way of producing large amounts of crops, by using chemicals and machines.

Mad Cow Disease

Bovine spongiform encephalopathy (BSE) is a disease that affects adult cattle, attacking the brain and *central nervous system* of the animal, eventually causing death. Many scientists believe that there are links between eating meat from cows with BSE and a serious human disease known as Creutzfeldt-Jakob Disease (CJD), a degenerative, fatal brain disorder that typically affects elderly adults.

Cattle graze in a field of buttercups near Stirling Castle, Scotland. Northern England and Scotland had the highest rates of Mad Cow Disease at the height of the problem in the late 1990s. Government controls over the beef industry in the United Kingdom seem to have gotten the problem under control.

This food inspector is testing the quality and safety of coffee beans.

Outbreaks of BSE throughout much of the 1990s in the UK devastated the cattle industry. More than 4.6 million older British cows were slaughtered to prevent the disease from spreading. In 1995, there were 14,562 cases of BSE, which went down to 1,443 cases in 2000 and 11 cases in 2010.

New laws require that only cattle under the age of 30 months can be used as food. Feeding any farm animal with material that includes processed body parts of sheep or cattle is now banned in the UK, as this is believed to have been one of the causes of the disease's spread.

The Difficulty of Monitoring Food Safety

There are tens of thousands of food products available to consumers, with many more being introduced every year. Each product can use many ingredients and many different processes in its manufacture. In addition, an individual food product may be produced in a number of different locations in a variety of batches and sent to multiple markets. Trying to keep track of all the foods, ingredients, additives, and processes used to make foodstuffs involves a vast amount of work.

Food hygiene, safety, and health agencies in many countries are simply overwhelmed with work and often do not have the staff or funding to investigate all these foodstuffs or visit the many thousands of food factories, distributors, and retailers that exist. In addition, the food standards and laws in different countries can vary greatly, making the tracing of food ingredients from overseas especially difficult.

Because food from one source can be distributed all over a large country or, further still, to many different countries, outbreaks of an illness can appear to be unrelated. In 1998, some 100 cases of Listeria, which caused 22 deaths in the United States, appeared to be unrelated, but through investigations,

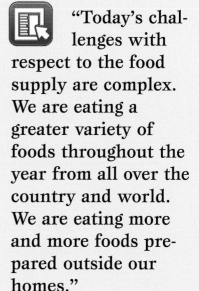

"Today's challenges with respect to the food supply are complex. We are eating a greater variety of foods throughout the year from all over the country and world. We are eating more and more foods prepared outside our homes."

—Jane E. Henney, former commissioner, US Food and Drug Administration they were traced to hot dogs and sliced meats manufactured by one factory. Food agencies in many wealthier countries are starting to use information technology to communicate food safety issues and to trace food problems back to their source. For example, the United States has established Pulse Net, a computer network linking public health laboratories to one another all over the country. It acts as an early warning system for outbreaks of foodborne disease.

The Need for More Scientific Research

Our knowledge of food and health is far from complete. For example, we do not yet know the full extent of the effect of some modern food additives on the human body over a long period of time. Nor do we fully know the effects of *intensive farming* and eating GM food on people or the environment. Every year, new food technology techniques and products reach the market. While some testing is performed on these new foods and techniques during the approval process, many experts believe that not enough long-term studies are being conducted to measure the effects of modern food on people's health.

The Progress of Campaigners for Food Consumers

Dozens of campaign and pressure groups exist in countries, and many are growing in strength as large numbers of people lose confidence in the safety and standards of food. Many groups have campaigned heavily in Europe against GM foods,

Scientists are continuing to test GM foods and their long-term effects on the people that consume them.

and although there have been crop trial sites, no GM crops are currently commercially grown in the UK or in a number of other EU nations.

There have been other successes. For example, following public pressure, battery cages for egg-laying chickens were banned in Switzerland in 1991 and more recently in Germany and Sweden. In the UK, after being highlighted by a number of consumer groups, the bleaching of flour to make it whiter using a chemical called benzoyl peroxide was banned in 1997. However, the chemical is still widely used in many other countries.

The Importance of Labeling

Labels are designed to inform consumers about what is contained within the food they are buying, so a customer can make a decision based on its ingredients. Some consumers may wish to choose a foodstuff that does not contain a specific ingredient for health or other reasons. Labels that have "use by" or "sell by" dates can also offer assistance in food safety.

Many food safety pressure groups are concerned that labeling laws in many countries are not strict enough. In many cases, they argue, labels are unclear, misleading, or not completely accurate. For example, in Europe, all foods containing GM ingredients must be labeled so that shoppers know what they are buying. However, amounts below one percent of GM material in foods need not be labeled. The United States does not have any laws that require labeling of any GMOs in food products. In the UK, a number of unwrapped foods, such as breads, foods from a cooked food counter, or sweets, do not have to carry ingredient lists, although any main additives must be publicly displayed on a ticket or notice nearby. In practice, this is not always done.

 # Text-Dependent Questions

1. What is the function of the HACCP?
2. Write two victories campaigners have had in fighting for the rights of food consumers to have healthy and safe food standards?

 # Research Project

Using the Internet or your school library, research the topic of food labeling, and answer the following question: "Should food companies be required to label all information about a food product?"

Some contend that all information should be on labels because the consumer has a fundamental right to know exactly what they are buying and eating, right down to the smallest quantity of an ingredient. One hundred percent accurate and complete labeling would force food manufacturers to trace every element of their food-production process.

Others argue that food companies should not have to label everything about a food product, just the main pieces of information, as too much information would confuse the public. Even if listed, most people would not recognize the names of chemical additives or understand what they are. Labeling every single ingredient, including ones that only have tiny amounts in a food, might be difficult and expensive for manufacturers, who would then pass the cost on to consumers.

Write a two-page report, using data you have found in your research to support your conclusion, and present it to your class.

The Future of Food Technology

No one can predict with certainty what the future holds for food technology and the food industry, but some trends are likely to continue for many years to come. Among these are further demands from many consumers for greater choice, lower prices, and foods that fit in with their lifestyle. Food safety, hygiene, how foods are produced, and what ingredients and additives they contain are also likely to become bigger public issues.

The Growing Food Safety Issue

People are becoming increasingly informed about the food they eat, their personal nutritional requirements, and their diet. Major issues, such as the BSE crisis and the hand, foot, and mouth outbreak, as well as the debate on GM foods, have

In some European countries, such as Germany, genetically modified organisms (GMO) must be clearly labeled so that consumers know what they are purchasing.

raised the public's awareness of issues about food in general. At the same time, the populations of many of the world's developed nations are becoming increasingly overweight on average while more money is being spent by health organizations in these countries to promote information about eating well and staying healthy.

New safety technology is likely to continue to be introduced for many foods. For example, a Canadian company, Toxin Alert, invented a plastic wrapper coated with chemicals that change color if they come into contact with a number of bacteria that cause foodborne illnesses, including Salmonella and E. coli. On the other hand, many campaign groups believe that it will take more than extra technology to stem the large number of foodborne illnesses that occur. They believe that far stricter laws on food safety and hygiene as well as greater punishments for those who break the laws will be required if food is to become safer.

Organic Foods

Alternatives to intensively farmed foods that use large amounts of chemicals and processing do exist, particularly in

 Words to Understand in This Chapter

biofuel—a fuel composed of or produced from biological raw materials. Wood is a biofuel; so is ethanol, a gasoline additive that is distilled from plants.

produce—fresh fruits and vegetables.

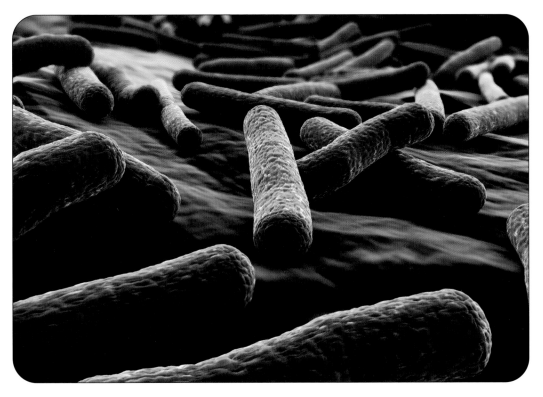

E. coli bacteria under a microscope. Only certain stains of E. coli are harmful, but to avoid them, meat has to be cooked thoroughly and high levels of hygiene practiced in kitchens.

the form of organic foods. Organic farms may still use high-tech equipment, such as mechanized harvesters, but they avoid the use of chemical pesticides, fertilizers, and GMOs. Supporters of organic farming maintain that the food produced is healthier, and the farm soil is kept in better condition.

Food that is organically grown is frequently more expensive because it is not produced in such large quantities as crops grown on large-scale farms. However, if organic farming were practiced on a larger scale, the price gap between factory-farmed and organically farmed *produce* would shrink greatly.

The USDA established national standards for organic production and processing in 2002. This gave specific requirements on how food could be produced and treated in order to be called "organic."

In 2012, the most recent year for which data is available, there were approximately $28 billion in organic food sales in the United States—about 4 percent of total at-home food sales. Produce such as fresh fruits and vegetables, along with dairy products, are the top two organic food categories, making up 43 and 15 percent, respectively, of total organic sales in 2012.

Like the USDA in the United States, there are also several organizations across the globe that have been established to monitor the production of organic food. In the United Kingdom, for example, the Soil Association oversees standards for the whole organic food industry. Its logo appears only on foods that have been produced according to rigorous standards. Products bearing this logo have been approved to offer consumers safe, nourishing food from healthy plants and animals.

The Outlook for GM Foods

Much depends on what advances are made and whether GM crops are accepted by governments and consumers worldwide, but genetically modified foods may have a major role in the food of the future. Crops which generate their own pesticides could reduce farming's reliance on harmful chemicals. Foods may be grown that manufacture large amounts of vitamins and other nutrients which people need for a healthy diet. As mentioned previously, GM golden rice is being developed for Asia, the home of 90 percent of the world's grown rice.

The future may also see genetically modified animals and plants turned into biological factories which produce incredibly useful substances, such as vaccines for diseases or *biofuels* that power motor vehicles. Opponents of GM foods believe that their impact on the food supply may not be so large, either because GM foods will remain unpopular with consumers or

Organic farming not only seeks to produce healthy food but also to create farming systems where animal welfare and care of the environment are priorities.

because a major environmental scare may prevent their further development.

Food Technology Going Forward

Food technology is unlikely to disappear. Food companies are too large, rich, and powerful to stop using the latest advances in food science to produce new foods—or old foods in new ways—in order to boost their profits. Demand is increasing for different-sized packages of food, as more people live on their own, and snack food sales may continue to rise with fewer people eating regular full meals.

As with all technological advances, those in the food industry can bring tremendous benefits to people all over the world, but critics point to such drawbacks as the economic impact on farmers, problems regulating food safety, and the amount of

 The Decaffeinated Coffee Plant

Caffeine is a drug found in coffee that can increase blood pressure and be harmful when consumed in large amounts, but taking the caffeine out to create decaffeinated coffee is an expensive process. *New Scientist* reported Japanese genetic engineers at the Nara Institute of Science and Technology have produced GM coffee plants that contain only 30 percent of the caffeine found in normal plants. They managed to switch off one of the genes responsible for generating much of the caffeine found in coffee. In this way, the future could see far cheaper and healthier decaffeinated coffee produced naturally.

waste produced. If the general public, along with campaigners, keep working to keep food-manufacturing companies accountable to putting people above profits, societies can reap many benefits while limiting the social, economic, and environmental costs.

 # Text-Dependent Questions

1. What new food safety technology was developed in Canada by Toxin Alert, and what does it do?
2. What are two benefits of organic foods over intensively farmed foods?

 # Research Project

Using the Internet or your school library, research the topic of organic versus conventional food, and answer the following question: "Should people choose organic over conventional food?"

Some think organic food is better because there are no pesticides or additives, which makes it healthier for people. The environment also does not suffer because of chemicals and massive plots of land used in conventional intensive-farming methods. Local farmers do not have to buy specific GM seeds and can sustain themselves in the long run.

Others say organic food is not any better than conventional food. There is no significant difference between them in terms of harm to humans because conventional foods still have to pass standards for levels of chemicals. Organic food companies try to scare the public into believing conventional foods are much more harmful than they really are. Conventional foods and GM foods often look and taste better, last longer, and are cheaper, so they are more beneficial to consumers.

Write a two-page report, using data you have found in your research to support your conclusion, and present it to your class.

Food Technology Statistics

Largest Food Manufacturing Companies in the World, by Sales

Company	Sales (in billions)	Products
1. PepsiCo Inc. (US)	$37.8	Beverages and snack foods
2. Tyson Foods (US)	33.0	Meat and poultry
3. Nestle (US/Canada)	27.3	Various
4. JBS USA (US)	22.1	Meat
5. Coca-Cola Co. (US)	21.6	Beverages
6. Anheuser-Busch (US)	16.0	Brewery
7. Kraft Foods Inc. (US)	14.3	Various
8. Smithfield Foods Inc.	12.5	Pork and beef products
9. General Mills Inc. (US)	12.5	Grain-based foods
10. ConAgra Inc. (US)	11.5	Various
11. Mars Inc. (US)	11.0	Confectionery

Company	Sales (in billions)	Products
12. Kellogg Co. (US)	9.7	Grain-based foods
13. Dean Foods Co. (US)	9.0	Dairy
14. Hormel Foods (US)	8.8	Meat and poultry, canned foods
15 Cargill Inc. (US)	8.5	Grain-based foods
16 MillerCoors LLC (US)	7.8	Brewery
17 Saputo Inc. (Canada)	7.8	Dairy
18 Pilgrim's Pride (US)	7.5	Meat, poultry, eggs, deli
19 Hersey Co. (US)	7.1	Confectionery
20 Mondelez (US)	7.0	Snacks, confectionery
21 Unilever (Neth.)	6.9	Grocery products, ice cream
22 Bimbo Bakeries (US)	6.1	Bakery goods
23 Dr. Pepper Snapple Group (US)	6.0	Beverages
24 J.M. Smucker (US)	5.6	Canned and preserved foods
25 Campbell Soup (US)	4.9	Canned and preserved foods

Source: *Food Processing's Top 100*, 2014

Causes of Foodborne Illnesses

Contaminant: Campylobacter

Onset of Symptoms: 2 to 5 days

Foods Affected and Means of Transmission: Meat and poultry. Contamination occurs during processing if animal feces contact meat surfaces. Other sources include unpasteurized milk and contaminated water.

Contaminant: Clostridium botulinum

Onset of Symptoms: 12 to 72 hours

Foods Affected and Means of Transmission: Home-canned foods with low acidity, improperly-canned commercial foods, smoked or salted fish, potatoes baked in aluminum foil, and other foods kept at warm temperatures for too long.

Contaminant: Clostridium perfringens

Onset of Symptoms: 8 to 16 hours

Foods Affected and Means of Transmission: Meats, stews, and gravies. Commonly spread when serving dishes do not keep food hot enough or food is chilled too slowly.

Contaminant: Escherichia coli (E. coli)

Onset of Symptoms: 1 to 8 days

Foods Affected and Means of Transmission: Beef contaminated with feces during slaughter. Spread mainly by undercooked ground beef. Other sources include unpasteurized milk and apple cider, alfalfa sprouts, and contaminated water.

Contaminant: Giardia lamblia

Onset of Symptoms: 1 to 2 weeks

Foods Affected and Means of Transmission: Raw, ready-to-eat produce and contaminated water. Can be spread by an infected food handler.

Contaminant: Hepatitis A

Onset of Symptoms: 28 days

Foods Affected and Means of Transmission: Raw, ready-to-eat produce and shellfish from contaminated water. Can be spread by an infected food handler.

Contaminant: Listeria

Onset of Symptoms: 9 to 48 hours

Foods Affected and Means of Transmission: Hot dogs, luncheon meats, unpasteurized milk and cheeses, and unwashed raw produce. Can be spread through contaminated soil and water.

Contaminant: Noroviruses (Norwalk-like viruses)

Onset of Symptoms: 12 to 48 hours

Foods Affected and Means of Transmission: Raw, ready-to-eat produce and shellfish from contaminated water. Can be spread by an infected food handler.

Contaminant: Rotavirus

Onset of Symptoms: 1 to 3 days

Foods Affected and Means of Transmission: Raw, ready-to-eat produce. Can be spread by an infected food handler.

Contaminant: Salmonella

Onset of Symptoms: 1 to 3 days

Foods Affected and Means of Transmission: Raw or contaminated meat, poultry, milk or egg yolks. Survives inadequate cooking. Can be spread by knives, cutting surfaces or an infected food handler.

Contaminant: Shigella

Onset of Symptoms: 24 to 48 hours

Foods Affected and Means of Transmission: Seafood and raw, ready-to-eat produce. Can be spread by an infected food handler.

Contaminant: Staphylococcus aureus

Onset of Symptoms: 1 to 6 hours

Foods Affected and Means of Transmission: Meats and prepared salads, cream sauces, and cream-filled pastries. Can be spread by hand contact, coughing and sneezing.

Contaminant: Vibrio vulnificus

Onset of Symptoms: 1 to 7 days

Foods Affected and Means of Transmission: Raw oysters and raw or undercooked mussels, clams, and whole scallops. Can be spread through contaminated seawater.

Source: Mayo Clinic, *Food Poisoning: Causes*

Organizations
to Contact

Center for Food Safety

660 Pennsylvania Avenue, SE, #302

Washington, DC 20003

http://www.centerforfoodsafety.org/

**International Service for the Acquisition
of Agri-Biotech Applications**

105 Leland Lab

Cornell University, Ithaca

New York 14853

http://www.isaaa.org/default.asp

Centre for Research on Globalization (CRG)

PO Box 55019

11 Notre-Dame Ouest

Montreal, Qc, H2Y 4A7

http://www.globalresearch.ca/theme/science-and-medicine

Institute of Food Technologists

525 West Van Buren Street, Suite 1000

Chicago, IL 60607

https://www.ift.org/

Organic Trade Association

444 N. Capitol Street NW, Suite 445A

Washington, DC 20001

https://www.ota.com/

US Food and Drug Administration

10903 New Hampshire Avenue

Silver Spring, MD 20993

http://www.fda.gov/

US Department of Agriculture

1400 Independence Avenue, S.W.

Washington, DC 20250

http://www.usda.gov/wps/portal/usda/usdahome

World Health Organization

525 23rd Street, NW

Washington, D.C. 20037

http://www.who.int/en/

National Institutes of Health

9000 Rockville Pike

Bethesda, Maryland 20892

http://www.nih.gov/

Wellcome Trust Sanger Institute

Hinxton, Cambridge

CB10 1SA, UK

http://www.sanger.ac.uk/

Series Glossary

apartheid—literally meaning "apartness," the political policies of the South African government from 1948 until the early 1990s designed to keep peoples segregated based on their color.

BCE and CE—alternatives to the traditional Western designation of calendar eras, which used the birth of Jesus as a dividing line. BCE stands for "Before the Common Era," and is equivalent to BC ("Before Christ"). Dates labeled CE, or "Common Era," are equivalent to *Anno Domini* (AD, or "the Year of Our Lord").

colony—a country or region ruled by another country.

democracy—a country in which the people can vote to choose those who govern them.

detention center—a place where people claiming asylum and refugee status are held while their case is investigated.

ethnic cleansing—an attempt to rid a country or region of a particular ethnic group. The term was first used to describe the attempt by Serb nationalists to rid Bosnia of Muslims.

house arrest—to be detained in your own home, rather than in prison, under the constant watch of police or other government forces, such as the army.

reformist—a person who wants to improve a country or an institution, such as the police force, by ridding it of abuses or faults.

republic—a country without a king or queen, such as the US.

United Nations—an international organization set up after the end of World War II to promote peace and co-operation throughout the world. Its predecessor was the League of Nations.

UN Security Council—the permanent committee of the United Nations that oversees its peacekeeping operations around the world.

World Bank—an international financial organization, connected to the United Nations. It is the largest source of financial aid to developing countries.

World War I—A war fought in Europe from 1914 to 1918, in which an alliance of nations that included Great Britain, France, Russia, Italy, and the United States defeated the alliance of Germany, Austria-Hungary, the Ottoman Empire, and Bulgaria.

World War II—A war fought in Europe, Africa, and Asia from 1939 to 1945, in which the Allied Powers (the United States, Great Britain, France, the Soviet Union, and China) worked together to defeat the Axis Powers (Germany, Italy, and Japan).

Further Reading

Cooper, James. *Food Myths Debunked: Why Our Food Is Safe*. Wilton, CT: Fairfield Easton Press, 2014.

Eschliman, Dwight, and Steve Ettlinger. *Ingredients: A Visual Exploration of 75 Additives & 25 Food Products*. New York: Regan Arts, 2015.

Lott, Joey. *Natural Deception: A Sobering Look at the Truth behind the Organic Food Industry*. Digital: Archangel Ink, 2015.

Lusk, Jayson. *Unnaturally Delicious: How Science and Technology Are Serving Up Super Foods to Save the World*. New York: St. Martin's Press, 2016.

Lustig, Robert H. *Fat Chance: Beating the Odds against Sugar, Processed Food, Obesity, and Disease*. New York: Hudson Street Press, 2012.

Mphil, Claire Robinson, Michael Antoniou, and John Fagan. *GMO Myths and Truths: A Citizen's Guide to the Evidence on the Safety and Efficacy of Genetically Modified Crops and Foods*. White River Junction, VT: Chelsea Green Publishing, 2015.

Internet Resources

www.fao.org

The home on the Internet of the United Nations (UN) Food and Agriculture Organization (FAO). One of the largest organizations within the UN, the FAO's website contains hundreds of web pages of statistics, articles, and reports.

www.foodhaccp.com

A large collection of hyperlinks to websites concerned with food technology and food safety.

www.foodsafety.gov

A gateway to many reports and frequently asked questions about food technology and food safety in the United States.

fsrio.nal.usda.gov

Homepage of the USDA's Food Safety Research Information Office, with dozens of links to issues concerning food safety, food technology, and the food industry in general.

www.gmnation.org.uk

This is the official website for the public debate over GMO foods, which took place in the UK in June, 2003. The website contains articles and opinions from all viewpoints.

www.ift.org

The homepage of the Institute of Food Technologists contains a wealth of information, including back issues of Food Technology magazine online.

www.monsanto.com/pages/default.aspx

One of the largest companies involved in biotechnology and GMO foods, Monsanto's home website is based in the United States and contains details of the company's products and research.

www.uk.foodtech.dk

A website designed for pupils and teachers interested in learning more about food processing and packaging in industry.

Index

Numbers in **bold italics** refer to captions.

About the Author

Chris Banzoff is a medical student at the Charles E. Schmidt College of Medicine at Florida Atlantic University in Boca Raton. This is his first book for young people.